MEDITERRANEAN
HOUSE

MEDITERRANEAN HOUSE

p

Fanny Blake

This is a Parragon Publishing Book
First published in 2002

Parragon Publishing
Queen Street House
4 Queen Street
Bath BA1 1HE, UK

Copyright © Exclusive Editions 2002

This book was created by Essential Books

A copy of the CIP data for this book is available from the British
Library upon request.

ISBN 1-84273-799-6

Printed in China

CONTENTS

INTRODUCTION

Square white houses basking in the heat of the day; town houses with peeling stucco facades; rough stone cottages lining a quayside—these are just some of the different images conjured up by the idea of the Mediterranean house. Having been seduced on vacation by the notion of a slower pace of life, a reliably sunny climate, and a more healthy lifestyle, even the most unadventurous decorator will be driven to recapture some of that magic in his or her own home. But with so many styles and details to choose from, where exactly to begin? Is it really possible to distill elements common to the architectures and interiors of the 17 different countries surrounding the Mediterranean basin and use them to bring the feel of a sunny and relaxed lifestyle into your own home? The answer is a definite "Yes."

It is the regional building materials that have dictated the design and appearance of houses in the different Mediterranean countries. Locally produced materials are relatively inexpensive and so are frequently used. Terra-cotta, stone, marble, stucco, and wood are among the most typical materials, but these alone will not evoke the style we are looking for. Many characteristic features of Mediterranean houses come from the climate, the cultures, and the lifestyles and these elements need to be brought into the design of the house too. The skilled craftsmanship that unites the many countries of the Mediterranean also brings with it the influences of Africa and Asia, seen, for example, in the rich traditions of wrought-iron work, wood carving, textile weaving, and ceramics. By using the right materials, and incorporating and adapting these traditional crafts into your own home, you will be able to create an authentic Mediterranean look.

Perhaps the most enviable thing about Mediterranean life is that so much of it takes place outdoors. Courtyards, roof terraces, verandas, porticos, and loggias are all features of the Mediterranean house. Porticos are covered areas at the front of the house, much like porches, and loggias are similar but at the side of the house. They provide additional living space and can be used effectively to shade the interior of the house. Large French doors and a continuation of the interior floor covering to the outside make for an easy flow of movement between interior and exterior. Outdoor

dining areas are often located near the kitchen for ease of access. Plants grow in profusion over trellis walls and roofs to provide welcome shade. Water plays from a fountain nearby. The table is laid and the scene is set for a day of relaxation and enjoyment. Nearby, a hammock swings invitingly in the breeze, waiting for siesta time.

The emphasis on life outdoors is reflected in the way the outside world is used within the home. Here, as elsewhere in the house, the emphasis is on simplicity, practicality, and the use of natural materials. Homage to the natural world is coupled with strong awareness of the past. Forget formality or state-of-the-art design. What furniture there is exists for a purpose and has often been handed down from one generation to another. Traditional crafts feature heavily, from time-honored hand-painted ceramics to woven rugs, brass lanterns, or heavy wrought-iron door and window hardware. Walls often reveal the march of time—a hint of nostalgia for times past goes a long way to creating the right effect.

Color plays a vital role in creating a Mediterranean-inspired living space. The use of vibrant colors in contrasting combinations characterizes all the different countries and regions of the Mediterranean. The particular quality of light of the Mediterranean intensifies the colors and brings a richness to the interior decoration.

Your choice of colors will be determined by the particular atmosphere you are hoping to re-create and the degree of intimacy you want to achieve. The impression of sunshine and light can be simply created with white walls and brilliantly colored accessories. A bright yellow will have a similar effect to white, while subtle color combinations can be used to evoke the warmth and exoticism of other regions.

Color is inseparable from pattern and texture. Wherever you are in the Mediterranean you will find distinctive patterns and textures in all the materials and furnishings in the house. The subtle patina of stone or tiled floors, the different grains of wood in chairs, tables, and doors, and the imperfections in natural finishes all contribute to the intrinsic character of a room. The bright weaves of rugs or wall hangings contrast with the plain white or yellow walls. Chair and pillow covers in different textures or fabrics contribute to the feel of the room.

The interior of the house tends to be open plan to encourage better air circulation. The family shares the single living space, which is centered primarily on the kitchen and dining area, where the most important item of furniture is the eternally adaptable sturdy wooden table. This is where the family begins and ends its day, gathering for a meal, helping with the preparation, exchanging gossip

Living in the open

One of the great pleasures of the Mediterranean lifestyle is being able to live outside. Nothing could be more pleasant than eating under a canopy of stars when the heat of the day has given way to a balmy evening. In the background, cicadas chirrup, the ocean murmurs in the distance, and the breeze whispers through the trees.

For centuries the people of the Mediterranean have used the space immediately outside their houses as another room. The Romans established the formal design of the inner courtyard that was sheltered both day and night from the heat of the sun and from any inclement weather by the surrounding building and the overhang of its eaves. Many houses are still built on this pattern. Courtyard living remains popular because the area is private, cool, and conveniently close to the kitchen when entertaining.

However, a courtyard is not the only option. Verandas are built out from upper floors with geraniums spilling from pots suspended on the railings, shaded by a canopy or split-cane blind. With a couple of chairs and a small table they can provide a vantage point which, if the view is good, will provide hours of quiet pleasure. Flat roofs lend themselves to being transformed into terraces if they are protected by a neighboring wall or overhanging eaves. A wooden trellis smothered with jasmine, a grapevine, or wisteria can shelter the area from the harshest sun.

The most common outdoor living space is obtained by extending the house into the garden, with a patio, a deck, or a covered balcony large enough to hold a table and chairs for alfresco dining. An important point to consider when adding a patio or deck is the direction in which it faces. If it is shady in the middle of the day, it may make a better breakfast area in the morning sun or a place for evening relaxing or entertaining. If it is particularly exposed, shade can be provided by using climbing plants on a trellis, which also offers an element of privacy.

All these outdoor spaces are essential for casual entertaining, ideal when friends come by on a summer evening or just as a private retreat for relaxation after a busy day.

opposite A sheltered porch provides the ideal spot for entertaining alfresco. It is ideally situated so that it spans the divide between the interior and exterior of the house, transformed into an outdoor room which can be used both day and evening.

below A split-cane canopy and a flourishing grapevine provide welcome shade from the sun while letting the light dapple through onto the table below.

Floors

Once you have planned the ideal position for an outdoor room, you must then think about its floor covering. Mediterranean style draws on natural materials so the choice is wide, though to an extent it depends on budget and on the finish of the adjoining house. Often an effortless continuity is achieved by using the same material as for the internal floors. For instance, stone slabs, terra-cotta tiles, and ceramic tiles can all be used both indoors and out, creating a natural flow between the two areas. Natural materials have an uneven finish, their varying tones providing additional interest in a uniform space. Whichever material is used, it must be both hard-wearing and weatherproof, able to withstand the onslaught of the elements. It may receive fairly rough treatment as furniture is moved over it and plates and glasses carried to and from the kitchen, as people gather for meals and sit late into the night to enjoy the balmy evening.

Using materials that contrast with the interior flooring can be effective too. Cobbles or large pebbles set in concrete are attractive, though not always the most practical when it comes to settling furniture on them.

left A traditional rush-bottomed chair and an old stone seat set against the varied tones of a slightly crumbling wall create just the right Mediterranean mood.

below *Wicker chairs can be arranged on a patio to provide a defined seating area. The use of natural materials and the simplicity of their design make them immediately and unobtrusively at home in the alfresco setting.*

They can be left natural or can be painted to create dazzling visual effects which can also be used to define different areas within the space, perhaps emphasizing a particular feature such as a flowerbed or fountain. Bricks can also be used to create different effects or to define areas by laying them in patterned sequences. You can underline a particular feature by changing the pattern of bricks around or under it—for example, in linear, herringbone, or other brick-bonding patterns. Wooden decks are another popular solution for those going for a Mediterranean look but wanting to avoid the expense of a natural stone finish. A deck offers all the possibilities of outdoor living and is easy to construct, attractive to look at, and extremely durable, though it may need some scrubbing to keep it at its best.

A Moorish or eastern atmosphere can be evoked by the use of colored mosaic/ceramic tiles. Rich patterns can again be used to pick out certain areas, emphasizing a particular color scheme, which might be echoed in the pottery or furnishings.

Walls

It is important to consider the walls adjacent to this special garden room. They can add to the atmosphere considerably if given the right attention. Brick and stone are obvious finishes since they need little maintenance and can age beautifully. On the other hand, it may be possible to re-create a Tuscan or Provençal feel by applying cement stucco and painting or limewashing it in a soft reddish or ocher shade. Or revisit that Spanish or Greek vacation experience by whitewashing the wall and offsetting it with brilliant blue in the furnishings and accessories. Mixing a calcimine paint with one of the colors of the Mediterranean palette is one way of achieving an instant and effective aged look. Paint finishes must be hard-wearing so that they don't need to be touched up too often. The added disadvantage could be that any repainting might be difficult when mature plants have grown up in the way. Sometimes it might be enough just to paint a section of one wall with a vivid blue, which can give the illusion of heat and sunshine.

Doors, window frames, and shutters all provide opportunities to add interest and color to the outside space. Bold contrasts can be made between wall and woodwork by using evocative colors that bring foreign lands to mind, be they the striking blue of Greece, the faded deep greens of Italy, or the earthier tones of the North African coast.

Light and shade

Although cooler climates tend to be less exhilarating than anywhere in the Mediterranean, they certainly have their good moments. There will be summer days when shade will be required against the hottest sun. If the patio or deck has a high adjoining wall, then it's relatively straightforward to attach an awning or canopy, possibly one that can be rolled or folded back on less

right *The bold stripe of the furniture fabric picks up the color of the walls and this is echoed in the canopy. The curved archway, antique wall lamp, and decoratively tiled steps are all typical Mediterranean features.*

clement days. The fabric can provide another way of adding atmosphere to the garden whether in an unadorned but sophisticated white or cream, a cheerful ice-cream shop stripe, or a subtle stripe on the edging, which can also be finished in a number of shapes—straight, scalloped, fringed, geometrical, and so on. It is also possible to build a lean-to roof which, supported by wooden or stone pillars, could be made of natural materials such as bamboo to provide an attractive variegated shade. Pergolas can also be effective close to the house and provide the perfect support for climbing plants that grow quickly up and over the supports. Combining a grapevine with jasmine results in dense shade and a divine scent that wafts through the garden both day and night. The same effect could be achieved by using sweet-smelling honeysuckle or even a swift-growing climbing rose. Wisteria is another climber that will provide some shade, with delicate mauve flowers hanging in profusion. If such an arrangement is too elaborate or the outdoor area is too far from the house, huge umbrellas can be moved around with the sun or can be placed in the center of a picnic table.

In the Mediterranean, long evenings are spent under the stars as the day cools down. As night falls, a gentle ambient light is needed that will retain the convivial atmosphere. Candles are the obvious answer. If it is a still and calm night, they can sit naked on the table, but why not choose from the huge variety of containers available? Containers will protect the flames from a breeze, and some styles will enable the candles to be hung around or over the table. Let a

opposite Built-in whitewashed stone seats are made comfortable and inviting with a scattering of colorful cushions and pillows in different fabrics.

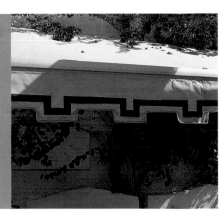

left The more simple and natural the furniture, the better. The small table looks like a sheaf of corn yet sits easily alongside the white cane chair by the pillar.

right The heavy white awning gives ample shade to this private seating area. The geometric edging with its dark trim adds a note of formality and neatly repeats the design of the stone seats.

subdued light shine out from the house while in the garden
itself various features, such as particular plants or statues, can be
highlighted with a spotlight hidden in nearby foliage. Lights can be
hung in the trees too but don't overdo it if you want to avoid the
taverna look. If using electric lighting in the garden, it should be
safety-approved and professionally installed.

Water

From the gentle lap of the ocean to the splash of a fountain in a
quiet courtyard, the sound of water is irrevocably associated with
the countries of the Mediterranean. Since the days of the Moors,
whose architectural influence is still felt so strongly in many parts
of the Mediterranean, water has been an important feature in any
outdoor planning. The sound and sight of water are instantly
soothing in the overwhelming heat of the day and create an
illusion of coolness in a shady retreat from the dusty outside world.
A simple bowl of water can be as effective as a larger pond or pool,
whose depths shimmer invitingly. A wall carving might have a
feature that spouts water into a container below. The sound of
water helps disguise any intrusive outside noise, reinforcing the
area's qualities of quiet and calm—an ideal place to get away from
it all and enjoy some solitude.

Plants

One feature that conjures up the Mediterranean perhaps more
than any other is the profusion of brilliant flowering plants that
brighten the outside of every house—the vivid purple of
bougainvillea, the pinks, reds, whites, and oranges of hibiscus
trumpets, or the lipstick red, baby pink, and white of geraniums.
Pots filled with brilliant-colored flowers that are easy to grow and
maintain will immediately lend an air of Mediterranean gaiety. Any
container that suits the style of its surroundings will do, including
smart clay pots, ceramic bowls, window boxes, hanging baskets, old
stone troughs, chimney pots, buckets, disused sinks, and even
painted oil cans. Plants can be bought from local nurseries, where

opposite and below The morning sun
shines down on a table set for breakfast.
Clay pots filled with leafy plants surround it to
give a sense of privacy and seclusion.

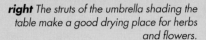

left *A simple table setting is brought to life by the addition of a bowl of tomatoes and a bunch of flowers.*

right *The struts of the umbrella shading the table make a good drying place for herbs and flowers.*

advice can be sought on the most appropriate plants to buy. With some sort of drainage system and enough water, they will flourish and immediately make a great impression.

Eating outside is one of the great pleasures of Mediterranean living. Make sure that the furniture suits the area without being too big or too small. Wooden furniture is practical and hard-wearing and looks good too. Covered with a white cloth and set with simple china and a vase of flowers, a utilitarian picnic table is transformed into a place for entertaining. Metal furniture can be less comfortable and may need some soft cushions—a good excuse for an additional splash of color. Mosaic or tile-topped tables give a bright surface that is as easy to clean as a marble top and both can be paired with simple metal chairs.

There's nothing quite like relaxing in a comfortable chair in the open air. Wicker armchairs or wooden chairs and sofas furnished with comfortable cushions can make all the difference to a shady roof terrace or a porch. Choose fabric colors to act as a contrast to or as part of the prevailing color scheme. These details are the finishing touches to make alfresco living fun.

opposite *A patio, deck, or porch is not an absolute necessity for enjoying life outdoors. When the sun shines take some chairs into the yard and create an instant outdoor room around an existing picnic table.*

Bold, vibrant colors used in striking combinations characterize the warmth and vitality of the Mediterranean countries. Extremes of light and shade play on every surface, creating intense and exciting variations in contrast and tone.

COLOR
AND LIGHT

The colors of the Mediterranean

One of the things that will strike you most on visiting any Mediterranean country is the quality of the light. The brilliant sun and frequently cloudless skies produce extremes of light and shade that intensify colors dramatically, presenting them at their most vivid and beautiful. Even the older, faded and crumbling ocher and terra-cotta stucco finishes on Italian houses have a heightened life of their own, thanks to the sun.

This exciting palette of contrasts is one influenced by and largely derived from the natural world. Traditionally dyes came from natural sources, using the natural pigments of the earth, plants, and even insects, and to this day this is reflected in the colors used in interior decoration all over the world. Chemical-based paints were introduced only midway

opposite and left *The striking contrast between blue and white immediately calls to mind the typical whitewashed villages that bask in the Greek island sun.*

through the 19th century. Until that time colors around the world belonged to the particular regions in which they were found.

There are effectively 13 essential colors that, when mixed with white, achieve huge tonal variations: yellow ocher, red ocher, raw sienna, burnt sienna, burnt umber, terra verde, and raw umber were derived from clay mixed with iron oxides and other mineral traces; ultramarine blue, copper blue and green, vermilion, and king's yellow or cadmium yellow make up the rest. Black came from carbon while white usually came from chalk or lime.

Most of these pigments are found all over the Mediterranean, where they can be seen used full strength in the bold combinations that characterize particular regions. The different regions along the Mediterranean coast have their own characteristic combinations of color. The most striking and perhaps the most memorable is the brilliant white of the Greek island houses set against the cerulean blue of the sky, which is echoed in their blue shutters and doors. Whether gleaming new or faded with time, the intensity of the blue always sets up a sharp, clean contrast, and when you use it in your own home, it will immediately evoke that part of the world. The colors of the southern coast of France tend to be more subtle, mixing rich deep reds with dark greens, varying shades of blue, and a sunflower yellow. Similarly, in Italy, the colors are muted, though no less intense, as the Italian sunshine beats on neighboring walls of terra-cotta, ocher, and deep green, with their shutters picked out in contrasting colors. Warm, spicy colors of turmeric and saffron yellow, peppery red, and nutmeg brown prevail on the

opposite A yellow, blue, and green color scheme is always reminiscent of summer days. Use these colors for accessories such as flowers, vases, and pictures as well as on walls and ceilings.

left Wicker furniture is brought to life with the use of cushions, pillows, and a striking floral throw. Blue and yellow work well together in conjuring up vacation memories of sunny skies.

right A delicate stencil of fresh green ivy leaves contrasts boldly with its surroundings and provides a link to the world outside.

below *The distressed blue-gray of the kitchen cupboard is cleverly tied in with the rest of the kitchen through the use of a simple stencil that echoes the color of the wall below.*

North African coastline, mixed with soft ochers, umbers, and siennas derived from the local clays, sometimes touched with a gleam of burnished gold.

Whatever their original derivations, these popular colors immediately evoke different aspects of Mediterranean life. Reds are reminiscent of clusters of geraniums tumbling from their pots, poppies swaying in a cornfield, ripe Italian tomatoes ready for picking, roasted red peppers shining in olive oil, the crisp flesh of watermelons, the rich deep red of local wines. Orange can range from that of fresh oranges picked from the tree or the velvety skin of apricots and peaches to the earthy terra-cotta of roof tiles baking under the sun and flowerpots crowded with plants. Yellow immediately brings to mind the strength of the sun beating relentlessly onto golden Mediterranean beaches, the zesty color of lemons displayed for sale by the side of the road, the soft creaminess of fresh butter from the farm, tall, proud sunflowers, and the glint of gold jewelry and brassware in the local markets. Different shades of green can evoke the silvery gray leaves of the olive groves, the shady green of the cypress trees, the variegated skins of mature melons, or the leaves of herbs. Blue immediately calls up the cloudless cobalt sky of Mediterranean summers, the aquamarine shallows of the ocean itself, the deeper blue of its depths, the delicate pale blue of plumbago flowers. Different intensities of purple bring fields of scented French lavender to mind as well as the shiny skins of eggplants piled high at the market, or dusky clutches of grapes ripe for collection. These are just some of the memories called up by the Mediterranean spectrum, not forgetting the dazzling white of the houses in Greece and southern Spain and the black of ripe olives, the priest's gown, and the inky night sky.

Experimenting with color

Re-creating a Mediterranean feel in the home depends on the judicious use of these strong, rich colors so that their vibrant combination will convey the warmth and romance so particular

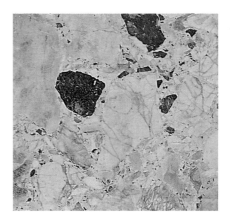

above *The variation in colors and pattern on a piece of marble is more fascinating and intrinsically beautiful than anything man could fabricate.*

below *Pale cream mugs hanging below the cupboard soften the division between the blue-gray of the cupboard and the pale yellow wall.*

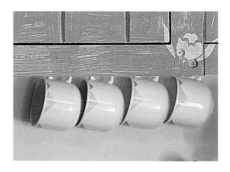

to this part of the world. When choosing a color scheme, it's important to take into account that the quality and variations of light in Mediterranean countries can be quite different to those in less sunny climates. The intensity of a particular color may be affected and seem less striking. The swatches of color on paint charts seem darker when the paint is used over a large expanse so it's always worth experimenting until you are absolutely certain the shade is the right one. By setting up contrasting colors side by side, life is often breathed into the more subdued of the two. If you are unsure which colors will work together to give you the desired effect, travel books that feature the Mediterranean countries will provide plenty of inspiration for colors and suitable accessories.

Take into account the size of the room in question. Small rooms will look smaller if the walls are painted a strong color. This may be appropriate for a warm and intimate atmosphere, particularly in a room such as a bedroom or dining room, but can be less appropriate if the room is frequently used by lots of people. Instead, it may be better to use a plain bright white but to set it off with just a band of color or a decorative wall stencil or by brightly painting the doors and window frames in a translucent blue or bright yellow. It is also possible to produce the right effect with just a suggestion of color on the ceiling or as an outline surrounding an archway or door. Another way of making sure you get a place in the sun rather than an igloo is by choosing bright accessories such as pillows, tablecloths, or rugs.

Maximizing light

The amount of natural light entering the room will largely determine the feel of the interior. Light is what we associate with the Mediterranean life and is essential if bold color schemes are to be seen at their daytime best. If the light is limited, consider ways in which it can be maximized. The most drastic course of action would be to make structural changes by knocking out a new window, enlarging an existing one to create French doors, or opening rooms up by removing dividing walls or creating an open mezzanine floor, to give additional height and space.

above Blue, green, and yellow: colors that connect us to the natural world of cloudless blue skies and translucent waters, green leaves and golden sunshine.

below Windows are rarely curtained. In this case a blind folds back so discreetly as to be barely there, letting maximum light stream in.

below *White and deep blue make a classic combination that brings Mediterranean buildings to mind. The windows are painted in white gloss which, thanks to the absence of curtains, reflects more light into the room. The green table and palest yellow walls add an extra touch of warmth.*

However, if such action is out of the question, there are other tricks that can be used to brighten a room. First and most obvious is to make sure the windows are properly cleaned. Curtain poles should extend beyond the windows so that curtains can be pulled right back, and furniture should be positioned so that it does not block the light. If a window has to be covered, consider using Venetian or split-cane blinds, or a light muslin curtain or shade, any of which will admit some light. As an alternative, etch-effect spray or stick-on etch-effect vinyl, though not ideal in this Mediterranean-style retreat, will at least allow some light to filter in.

above *Muted shades of blue, pink, and yellow combine to create an effect reminiscent of a new dawn breaking over the horizon.*

left *A brick floor weathers with age into a mellow terra-cotta. Brighter contemporary accents are provided by plenty of different flower arrangements.*

above *White is the predominant color in this room, thanks to the furnishings and the generous picture mats, although the pink of the walls is picked up in the design of the vines on the sofa fabric. The blue shutters provide a striking contrast.*

Use reflective surfaces to enhance what light there is in the room. Mirrors can be used to make a room seem bigger. Large wood- or gilt-framed ones can be propped up against the wall, giving a slightly Turkish or Italian feel, or smaller ones can be hung. Windows and doors should be painted with gloss paint in preference to eggshell because the finish will bounce light back into the room. The varnish on a wooden floor or on wooden furniture will have a similar effect. Tiles provide another reflective surface that can, depending on their color, have the same effect. Frequently used in kitchens and bathrooms, tiles can also be effective in a living room where, for example, they might be used on a mosaic tabletop or even on the floor.

When trying to boost the available light, the room should be kept as uncluttered as possible, with the amount of furniture kept to a minimum. Pale fabrics can be lifted with a splash or two of color from a throw or scatter pillows. Bookshelves, and shelves in alcoves, should have spaces left on them so the wall behind is visible, increasing the illusion of space and light. Whatever furniture is already in the room may dictate the

style and colors that are used in its decoration. Pine particularly calls for the bright whites and blues of Greece, or the yellows and reds of Provence, while heavier, more traditional furniture might go better with the more opulent schemes of Turkey or Italy.

When night falls

Candles are frequently used in the Mediterranean home, placed directly on the dining table, held in wall sconces, or floating in a bowl of water. Candlelight immediately recaptures the essence of those balmy outdoor evenings that have become mere memories. Their gentle glow can be augmented with the stronger but equally mellow light from oil lamps, all of which will be reflected in the shiny surfaces of the room. There is a great variety of ornamental lanterns and chandeliers that use candles and would add an original finishing touch. Some of these are authentic while others are copies of designs from Europe and Africa.

Electric lighting must be carefully controlled if it is to provide the right atmosphere. Dimmer switches are a must because they will give flexibility and can be adapted to suit the occasion. Glaring overhead lights will kill the effect stone dead. Far better to choose discreet uplights or wall sconces to provide a subtle but warm ambient light, with focus given to a particular treasure or area by a direct spotlight. Table lamps can be placed around the room, introducing a touch of color through the bases and shades. To fit in with the Mediterranean atmosphere, these should have an aura of age about them, even if they have only recently been distressed with a scrape of sandpaper and a glaze.

Achieving a Mediterranean style is about creating an illusion. Having considered the size of the particular room, the available day and night light, and the furniture that will be used, it is possible to choose the appropriate contrasting colors to conjure up another part of the world where the sun always shines and the living is easy.

left *Louvered shutters are commonplace along the Mediterranean. They keep rooms cool by barring the sun while admitting breezes. Painted in bold colors, they make a striking feature on any house.*

The kitchen is central to Mediterranean family life. Complete with plenty of open storage, a large, well-scrubbed pine table in the center, and diverse freestanding cupboards, it is a hive of activity that is always warm and inviting.

MEDITERRANEAN KITCHEN

above *French doors opening onto a porch from the kitchen make the most practical solution for outdoor entertaining. Food and wine can be carried to and from the table with the minimum amount of fuss while the host remains in earshot and can continue to share the conversation.*

The heart of the home

Juicy sliced tomatoes glistening under a drizzle of olive oil, saffron seafood risotto or Spanish paella bubbling on the cooktop, huge pans of boiling pasta with the whiff of garlic and basil in the air, rich meat daubes and carbonnades, fish baking in the oven or sizzling in a large frying pan, bright fresh vegetables awaiting preparation—these are just some of the culinary and visual delights to be found in a Mediterranean kitchen, and are what gives it such a distinctive feel.

The kitchen is traditionally the heart of the home, and the Mediterranean kitchen is no exception. It is always full of activity. Warm and comfortable, it is a place toward which friends and family naturally gravitate. It is characterized by the appetizing smells that emanate from it day and night, as newly gathered fruit and vegetables, herbs, fresh fish, and meat are transformed into delicious meals. It may have modern appliances but its appeal is centuries old and marked by simplicity of detail and the use of natural materials.

If your kitchen is being designed from scratch, first look at what you're working with. Consider the size and scale of the room in question. For example, it will be much harder to inject an intimate Mediterranean feel into the kitchen of a period town house than it will into a low-ceilinged country cottage, although there are features that will still convey the appropriate atmosphere, if used carefully. Lower the ceiling, or create the feeling of a lower ceiling by installing hanging utensil racks, which can also be used for drying flowers and herbs. Paint the ceiling a darker color, or use lighting to pick out the furnishings without emphasizing the height of the room. Look for any existing features that particularly stand out, such as a beam that can be exposed or a fireplace that can be used as a focal point. The homeyness of a roaring log fire on a cold winter's night cannot be matched.

Natural light is an essential. The direction the house is facing will dictate the amount of light a room receives at any particular time during the day. If light is limited, look at the ways it could be

above *Majolica tiles are extremely popular for kitchen decoration. A glaze of tin oxide gives the clay tile an opaque white surface which contrasts with the brightly painted patterns, bringing a splash of Mediterranean sun into the home.*

maximized, perhaps by adding an extra window, French doors, or even a skylight. Remember that there are practical considerations as well when designing your kitchen. Fridges, freezers, microwaves, washing machines, and dishwashers may need to be incorporated into the layout of the kitchen without spoiling the desired traditional look. Instinct or modern design solutions may dictate that a large work surface is needed but too large a surface may mean that space will be sacrificed for other, more idiosyncratic and interesting pieces of freestanding furniture, such as armoires, dressers, or cupboards. It may be enough for the cook to have access to a central island or, more traditionally, a table. Having worked out the must-haves in your kitchen, have fun creating the warmth and atmosphere of a real Mediterranean kitchen around them.

Kitchen flooring

Floors are commonly paved with large, well-scrubbed flagstones or warm terra-cotta tiles. The stone used for kitchens tends to be sandstone or limestone, both of which are cool and stylish, working well in both contemporary and traditional surroundings, as their variable textures and colors add interest to any style of interior. Because of the porous nature of these stones, both stain easily but can be protected with sealant or polish, though this may make the surface more slippery. Bear in mind the weight of the flags, which make them unsuitable for anything other than a ground floor. Reproduction stone is available and, while much

left *The family can gather for meals at a large centrally placed rustic table. A tablecloth adds a touch of color that ties in with the backsplash and readies the table for entertaining.*

below *The wooden units, open shelves, and tiled backsplash are hallmarks of the Mediterranean kitchen. Utensils and china are kept easily accessible, their shapes and colors adding a simultaneous decorative flourish.*

above Hints of the Mediterranean can be brought into an urban kitchen by drying herbs or by hanging strings of appropriate vegetables with utensils on a ceiling rack.

cheaper than the real thing, it is rarely as effective. It is important to keep the scale of the room in mind—large flagstones work best in a large space. Terra-cotta tiles are the oldest hard tiles available. They age very well to give a subtle, warm glow that immediately infuses the atmosphere. The colors of these tiles can vary in intensity, depending on their origin, from the pink or yellowish tiles of Provence to the richer shades of Tuscan terra-cotta. Bricks laid in herringbone and basket-weave patterns or in staggered rows can make another highly pleasing alternative.

All these natural flooring materials have the advantage of providing a cool surface in the summer heat and some natural cooling in pantries and storerooms. They have an unpretentious, informal appeal and as years go by become even more attractive as they are worn to a smooth patina by countless generations walking over them. Stone is now fairly expensive and sometimes difficult to obtain, but architectural salvage yards may be a source of secondhand flagstones, tiles, and bricks that have been recovered from old country houses or farms. If this is too expensive or impractical a solution, wooden flooring is a sound natural alternative and of course infinitely more practical than stone if the kitchen is not on the ground floor.

Wall treatments

In an old building, the original stone walls and wooden beams can be left exposed, as the texture and patterns of the stonework make a striking feature. But in a more modern house, where the illusion of Mediterranean life needs to be slightly more subtle, it is important to plaster and then paint the walls the right color. White will make the most of the available light and conjure up an atmosphere of airy sunshine, which can also be evoked by using a bright yellow. Although rarely seen in authentic Mediterranean kitchens, it wil create the desired illusion of sun and heat in a kitchen subjected to a more subdued northern climate. A soft terra-cotta or one of the natural earth colors can also capture the warmth of the Mediterranean landscape without

left *Yellow and green shelves bring the sunshine into the kitchen, acting as a strong backdrop to the subtle tones and shapes of the pottery and vegetables.*

forfeiting too much light. As an alternative, there are various specialist plaster and paint finishes that can be used to fake a natural, aged look (see WALLS AND FLOORS). Make the most of the existing doors and windows. French doors that lead to a porch, patio, or deck for outdoor dining are ideal, providing easy access from the kitchen and increasing the sense of light and space.

Wall tiles are another must. For centuries, Mediterranean countries have used handmade ceramic tiles for decorative as well as practical purposes. Spain, Portugal, and Turkey have all been particularly known for their individual styles, which were exported all over the world (see TILES AND CERAMICS). Waterproof, easy to clean, and a great source of color, they are ideal for backsplashes and countertops, as well as floors. Some people, however, find that the uneven surface of tiles makes them difficult to work on. Also, the grout can be hard to keep clean, but there are types of grout available that do not absorb bacteria and make dirt easy to wash away. Otherwise, tiles can be used to decorate the lip of the countertop, the curve of an archway, or the edge of a window frame. The Portuguese are famed for their walls tiled from top to bottom. Let your imagination tell you when to stop!

Kitchen furniture

The centerpiece of the kitchen is the table. A marble-topped one is ideal for preparing food and rolling pastry, but more commonly a large, sturdy wooden table is placed in the middle of the room and used by all the family. It is not just for eating meals but also for such activities as doing homework, reading the papers, writing letters, unpacking the shopping, rolling pastry, chopping and peeling fruit and vegetables,

above *Terra-cotta, sunshine yellow, and cream color schemes are very suitable for a Mediterranean-inspired house. A splash of leaf green complements them well and provides a refreshing contrast.*

opposite *The large windows are left unobstructed to maximize the light entering the room, so that counters are well lit during the day and a pleasure to work at.*

left *The sinuous curves of the wrought-iron chairs set up a contrast with the geometry of the rest of the kitchen, softened further by the addition of check cushions.*

right *A terra-cotta floor has subtle variations in tone which come to life as the sun and shade move over them.*

kneading bread dough. The surrounding chairs are often mismatched—rush-seated, Windsor, or ladderback will all do the trick. Consider using chairs that aren't intended for the kitchen, such as wicker chairs from the yard, metal folding chairs, or wrought-iron outdoor chairs. Providing them with cushions in a sunshine print from Provence, a bold deckchair stripe, or a subtle check will immediately add a vital splash of color to the room. If the space is large enough, a sofa or somewhere to perch adds an inviting, friendly touch.

The kitchen furniture should all be as simply designed as possible and preferably made from wood. Change the doors on existing cabinets if necessary and add wrought-iron handles and drawer pulls for a Mediterranean touch. Countertops should ideally be wooden or tiled in order to be both practical and hard-wearing and should include a shallow sink or an apron sink. Freestanding storage is particularly characteristic of the Mediterranean kitchen. Scour antiques fairs and garage sales to find furniture that can be given a new lease on life in the kitchen.

left *A sense of abundance is what you are aiming for. Here there is a good deal going on, with pots, pans, herbs and spices, and accessories, but the kitchen still retains a neat and fresh feel.*

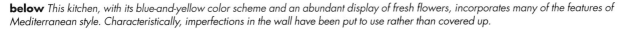

below *This kitchen, with its blue-and-yellow color scheme and an abundant display of fresh flowers, incorporates many of the features of Mediterranean style. Characteristically, imperfections in the wall have been put to use rather than covered up.*

A kitchen of plenty

The Mediterranean kitchen is not a place for minimalism, with utensils packed out of sight in neat cabinets. Old armoires should groan under the weight of the pots and pans inside, while glass- or chickenwire-fronted cupboards and open shelves display piles of plates, nests of bowls, and rows of pitchers. Mugs hang from hooks while cooking utensils are all on open display, whether stuffed into earthenware jars or hanging from ceiling beams, from a ceiling rack, or on the wall alongside serving platters and trays. String a metal cable along the wall and use meat hooks to hang up colanders, pans, copper molds, and so on. Meanwhile, plates can live in open wooden plate racks above the draining board. Everything is in view and within easy reach.

The ideal stove for a Mediterranean-style kitchen is a provincial French-style range, which can combine gas and electricity (handy in a power cut), has great rustic charm, and provides plenty of room for all those cooking pots. Traditional freestanding stoves can also fit in with the mood, as can a discreet built-in oven and a good cooktop.

If you have conventional built-in cabinets, then it's perfectly possible to create a Mediterranean-style kitchen with accessories, all of which should be functional as well pleasing to the eye. Make a point of displaying crockery. There's no need to travel to the Mediterranean to buy attractive ceramic pottery plates and bowls. Plenty of specialist shops and department stores stock a wide range. Mix and match the patterns and styles. Marble pastry slabs have a pleasing solidity and coolness. Terra-cotta containers and wicker baskets are typical Mediterranean accessories. Use them to hold vegetables and fruit or just pile them up in a corner.

Fruit and vegetable displays on the counter—a simple bowl of lemons or a colorful mix of eggplants, onions, and bright red bell peppers—give a lush feel to the kitchen. Herbs can be grown in window boxes indoors. Hang bunches of dried herbs and lavender from the ceiling, between the pots and pans on a hanging rack. Strings of garlic and onions can join them. Line the shelves with glass jars of preserved fruit, bottles of vinegar and olive oil (decant store-bought oil into attractive containers), spice racks, jars of flour and sugar, and so on. The key is not to worry if things do not line up in uniform rows. The Mediterranean look depends on asymmetry and a variety of pleasing shapes, patterns, and textures. Open shelves can even be finished off by pinning heavy lace borders to each one. Cover the table with a check cloth, choosing a color that echoes another element in the kitchen such as the tiles or cushions. As a final touch, add a bunch of wildflowers.

In the evening, make sure that the work surfaces are effectively lit and that the table is well illuminated, possibly with a central pendant light. Then, for that extra bit of Mediterranean magic, light candles around the room and the scene is set.

above Subtle pinks against a cream background are lifted by the addition of a sharp violet. Such vivid combinations work well over a small area, particularly when set against the white of the rest of the kitchen.

left A simple spongeware salad bowl has a practical function but it can also be used as a decorative object on its own.

right A floral shade provides an apt reminder of the natural world. By keeping the design simple, it can be pulled right up out of the way on a sunny day.

above The view out to the weathered brickwork is pleasingly softened by the addition of many plants, both indoors and out. Geraniums spilling from clay pots add those all-important Mediterranean splashes of color.

Houses basking in the Mediterranean sun are deliberately designed to be cool indoors. Thick walls, high ceilings, and paved or tiled floors all help achieve this aim. The emphasis is on natural materials left unadorned or simply decorated to reflect the colors and the textures of the world outside.

WALLS AND FLOORS

below The rough plaster walls act as a natural foil for the deep terra-cotta floor and the grain of the wood. The wooden pillar supporting the beam where the room has been expanded into a kitchen/dining room has its own particular charm.

The interiors of Mediterranean houses are designed to be cool. Walls are thick, windows small and usually shuttered. Ceilings are high and floors are paved with stone, tiled, or boarded. The Mediterranean house is designed to offer welcome respite and a cool haven from the often intense heat of the day. This is achieved by the unaffected use of natural materials that make the link between the interior and the outside world. The patterns and textures of these natural materials are decoration enough, whether in the form of the play of light and shade on a rough stone wall, the varying sheens of a well-trodden tiled ceramic floor, or the grain of exposed wooden beams and floorboards. As elsewhere in the Mediterranean house, the keyword when it comes to the walls and floors is simplicity.

Walls

You'll recognize the houses of particular regions immediately by their walls, whether these are colored Italian stucco, Greek or Spanish limewash, or the unadorned natural stone of southern France or Spain. Windows are frequently framed by shutters, which are either solid wood or slatted to let the light and air filter into the rooms. Both types of shutters can be painted in bold colors to contrast with the building, or painted more subtly to harmonize with it. Blue shutters and doors against white walls define many Greek homes; vivid or dark green shutters stand out against Italian siennas and terra-cottas; smoky blue contrasts with a

below The curved archway leading to the heavy front door is reminiscent of many Mediterranean interiors. It gives the impression of an extremely thick, protective outer shell.

right When structural beams are painted, they become less obvious, the ceiling seems higher, and the sense of space is increased.

Provençal red, and so on. The hinges and fasteners are often crafted in heavy metal so that when closed from the inside, the shutters provide reliable security.

Windows can also be protected by a metal screen or grille, as an alternative to shutters. These are particularly common in Spain where they can be extremely decorative. In days gone by, the amount of decoration was a testament to the wealth of the owners of the house, as well as providing extra protection from the outside. Doors are traditionally heavy and often decorated with studs or ornamental metalwork. These doors are found particularly on the outer walls of houses when they open onto an inner courtyard. Otherwise, outside doors are often brightly painted and welcoming, and are sometimes given added focus by a framing band of color instead of molding. The hinges, handles, and knockers are invariably heavy and frequently made of ornate wrought iron.

Indoors, the walls can be treated in a number of ways to capture the essence of Mediterranean living. Untreated stonework is an attractive natural finish, the texture of which adds immediate character and life to a room, linking it to the outside world. If the surface is felt to be too uneven or unfinished, it can be plastered then whitewashed. This is a simple solution adopted by many households. Often calcimine or limewash is used as a natural alternative to whitewash. Both of these are water-based and have served as a traditional wall covering for centuries, although they are most commonly used on the exterior of the house. They allow the

opposite *The exposed wooden beams, the colors and shapes of the hexagonal terra-cotta tiles, the roughcast wall covering, and the solid wooden door show how the outside world can be brought indoors to create a warm and inviting interior.*

left *Characteristic open shelves that seem to be carved out of the wall itself provide a good place to store and display traditional handicrafts.*

right *The delicate fabric of the curtain protects against the sun while allowing light to filter through into the room.*

building to "breathe" so there is little cracking or peeling. Even when plastered, the shapes of the underlying stones can show through and provide an excellent backdrop for the play of light and shade as the sun moves over them. White walls immediately give the impression of light, space, and coolness, even if smooth and flat. For added interest, the stone surround of the windows can be left exposed, or the doors and windows can be painted brightly in contrast.

When it comes to painting the walls there is a large palette of colors to choose from (see COLOR AND LIGHT), ranging from the pastels of the Italian Riviera to the traditional richer terra-cottas, siennas, and umbers. However, what typifies Mediterranean style above all is its enjoyment of history. The patina of age and the chips and dents that come with it are considered attractive, rather than something to be quickly retouched or repainted. Colors are bleached by the sunshine and acquire a character that is completely unique. In non-Mediterranean countries we can imitate this "distressed" look by using different specialist paint effects, such as sponging, dragging, or stippling, or by applying a subtle colorwash. Light will play over the different textures and tones to give an appropriately faded look.

The important thing to remember with colors is that the best results will be achieved by keeping the color scheme simple. Colors should be used in uninterrupted blocks so that they define a particular room or a space within a larger room. For the more artistic and adventurous who are fortunate enough to have space at their disposal, there is always the option of a trompe-l'œil painting. What better way to cheer up a dreary room or staircase than to create your own view of the rolling Tuscan countryside or the lavender fields of France?

As an alternative to exterior shutters, you could create an impression of Mediterranean style by bringing the shutters indoors so that they sit flush against the wall and, when closed, provide additional security. In Morocco, windows are often

right Contemporary radiators have no place in a warm climate. Where it is colder they can be boxed in behind a fretwork screen, leaving the room to appear sublimely cool.

screened to maintain the privacy of the women in a household. The fretwork screens have the same practical advantage as the shutters, filtering the light and heat entering the room. In a cool winter, heavy drapes or tapestries would once have been hung over the doors and windows to keep in the heat, which is an appropriate solution where the weather is colder. Traditionally, the curtains most associated with Mediterranean style are made from light, floaty fabrics such as muslin or voile. They partially shade the room but also let any breeze waft through into the interior.

Shelving is essential in the Mediterranean house. Alcoves and niches seem to be an intrinsic part of the walls and allow the easy display of anything from towels in the bathroom, through books in the living area, to ceramics or utensils and provisions in the kitchen. It is the unaffected, straightforward ease of access to everything that is a hallmark of the house. What usually happens is that when the Mediterranean house is designed and built, various alcoves or shelving units are actually planned as part of the walls and then painted to blend in with them. It is possible to create a similar effect by using the existing space in alcoves on either side of the fireplace, or in the dead space surrounding doors or under stairs. Otherwise, wooden shelves, either painted or perhaps treated in order to match floorboards or ceiling beams, are both practical and typical.

below *Curtains hung on a simple wooden pole can be drawn to prevent draughts in winter.*

right *White paint has been cleverly used to accentuate the distinctive features in this room. The built-in seats and the painted window surround are both typical Mediterranean features.*

opposite *Distressing the wall and painting the roof trusses white make them melt into the background, concentrating the eye on what is going on in the lower part of the room.*

Floors

Floors in the Mediterranean region have for centuries been covered with stones quarried locally, with wood from indigenous forests or terra-cotta tiles made from local clay. These natural materials all provide clean, cool surfaces that become more attractive with the patina of age, are long lasting, and are easy to clean. They also have the benefit of helping keep the house cool during the long summer months. Stone, slate, and marble are often used, as are terra-cotta tiles and bricks (see MEDITERRANEAN KITCHEN). Pebbles are another natural source of inspiration for Mediterranean flooring. Small or large pebbles are set in concrete to give a hard-wearing cobble finish. The deeper they are pressed into the concrete, the smoother the effect. They can be used close together or more widely spaced, and either left natural or painted, depending on the overall desired effect.

Another popular alternative is a wooden floor. Its appeal is timeless, and the style and appearance of a wooden floor suit almost any interior, giving a warm finish to a room. The grain and knots of the wood give it a vitality all of its own. As wood ages, it develops its own individual character. Different woods produce a variety of shades, textures, and patterns yet every one provides a coherent, unobtrusive background that can take a good deal of wear and tear. The presence of floorboards contributes to the sense of the natural world coming inside the house. Authentic old boards may be hard to come by but it is possible to use one of a number of techniques to weather them. They can be lightened by pickling— that is, rubbing white paint or paste wax into the grain of the wood—or they can be darkened by staining and varnishing, which lets the grain of the new wood show through but makes it appear more seasoned.

Wall-to-wall carpets have no place in the Mediterranean home, but rugs of any kind have a long history. They add warmth, color,

right There are a number of ways to distress paintwork to capture the patina of age. By reversing the effect on the radiator, it has been cunningly disguised to blend in with both the wall and the doors.

below *In a white room, take a principal contrasting color and use it to bring the room together. Here, the brilliant blue of the shutters is picked up in the many pictures and other accessories, while the white allows other flashes of color to add to the stunning overall effect.*

and a welcome sense of domesticity. Since rugs are movable, they do not tie you down to any permanent flooring arrangement and you can change them with the seasons, or to suit your mood. A rug adds depth and character to a room and can be used to define particular spaces—a sitting area may have chairs grouped around a rug or the rug may be used to define a path through a space.

Rugs are also often used as wall hangings, both for decoration and to stop drafts from badly fitting doors and windows. Turkey and North Africa are particularly famous for their knotted rugs and woven kilims, in which the rich reds, blues, blacks, creams, and golds derive from natural vegetable dyes. The luminosity of these carpets gives way with time to much softer but equally radiant shades. Any of these rugs lends immediate vitality to a room, whether they are used singly or laid one on top of another for the heady atmosphere of the bustling open-air marketplace (or "souk"). In Greece, woolly white or off-white shag-pile rugs are welcome on a chilly winter's night.

If you prefer a more neutral floor covering, there are plenty of easily available alternatives made from natural fibers such as seagrass, sisal, coir, or rush. Although these coverings are popular in contemporary design, they have a history that goes back centuries. They are not expensive and contribute to the natural feel of the home with the patterns and textures in their weaves. They are extremely versatile, ecologically sound, and pleasing to the eye. Most are reasonably hard-wearing, although they do have a tendency to stain and are not suitable for kitchen or bathroom areas, where any humidity may damage them.

When deciding how to treat the walls, ceilings, and floors in a Mediterranean-inspired home, always turn to the world of nature for inspiration. Keep things simple and unadorned, letting the variety and flexibility of the materials used in the fabric of the house speak for themselves.

above One way of defining a seating area is to frame the relevant section of terra-cotta floor tiles with a ceramic border that picks up the other colors in the room.

For centuries, tiles and ceramics have been a defining feature of Mediterranean style. They provide color and warmth with a practical, hygienic finish. Their presence immediately evokes happy days of sunshine and laughter.

TILES AND CERAMICS

For centuries tiles have been used all over the world both to decorate buildings and to provide a sound, practical, and hard-wearing finish to floors and walls. To this day, they continue to be a defining feature of Mediterranean homes. Tiles range from terra-cotta floor tiles that have mellowed with age through to bright ceramic tiles that enliven a bathroom or kitchen. Whatever type of tile you choose to use, it will provide a lively, vital finish to a room.

A brief history

Many Mediterranean cultures have played a part in the development of tile production. Glazed tiles were first used in ancient Egypt and the Near East. It was the potters of the Islamic world who were largely responsible for discovering new ways to fire and glaze tiles and this went on to influence tile production in the rest of the world. The Islamic potters frequently decorated their mosques by completely covering both the interior and exterior walls with complex patterns of tiles that gleamed brilliantly under the sun, so glorifying their places of worship. By the 16th century, Turkey was producing sensational color combinations of blues, greens, blacks, and whites, later adding a brilliant red. The tiles were largely produced at Iznik and Kütahya, where the designs of court artists were brought to life using the local clays and mineral dyes. Shapes of tiles varied. Alongside the square were the triangle, hexagon, pointed cross, and eight-pointed star. Patterns on the tiles were elaborate imitations of the natural world, created using motifs that typically appeared in rugs and textiles. The effects were dazzling.

The 13th century saw a boom in the tile industry in Moorish Spain, and Málaga became the center of the trade. The Alhambra in nearby Granada is a fine example of the art of tile-laying, with room after room displaying breathtaking patterns of interlocking geometric designs. Even outside in the courtyards the light sparkles off the tiled pools, floors, and pillars.

When the Moorish empire began to decline, many Islamic craftsmen remained in Spain and continued to expand the tile trade. Later, the center of production moved to Valencia.

opposite *Single tiles can be used decoratively inside as well as outside the kitchen. These floral tiles successfully hint at both the heavy stone floor and the natural world glimpsed through the window.*

below *Ceramic tiles make an ideal finish in any kitchen. They are attractive, easy to clean, and hygienic. Single decorative tiles can be inserted into a run of plain ones to add color and interest.*

Valencian tiles, which were used on floors, walls, and even rooftops, featured portraits and complex patterns. These tiles were shipped via Majorca to Italy, and subsequently became known as "majolica" tiles, even though they were not actually produced in Majorca. The Italians then developed the craft themselves, producing highly decorative floor and wall tiles.

During the 16th century the majolica technique reached its heights, and superb decorative tiles were produced in large quantities. Unlike in Spain, where tiles were used largely on walls and ceilings, in Italy they were used predominantly on floors. The penchant for these tiles spread farther afield to France, Austria, Germany, and Holland, and new factories were established.

Tiles are as popular a form of decoration in Mediterranean countries today as they were then. They have established themselves permanently in the domestic setting and are one of the most distinctive features of Mediterranean-style homes.

left *The Romans raised mosaic-laying to an art form. Today, methods have been greatly simplified and superb decorative effects can be achieved with surprisingly little effort.*

opposite *Far more than just a backsplash, tiles can be used to decorate large areas of wall. They are designed to be admired, whether looked at individually or in a group, and can be used to define the color scheme of a room, as in this kitchen.*

Tiling for floors

Tiles have been used on the floors of Mediterranean houses for generations. Their versatility and adaptability mean they can provide an understated, neutral background or can function as a striking focal point in a room. Although tiles are used to help the interior of the Mediterranean house stay cool, in a colder climate they are transformed by the addition of underfloor heating.

The clay necessary for the production of terra-cotta tiles is found all over the region. Introduced by the Moors to Spain between the 13th and 16th centuries, the tiles were soon produced throughout Europe. They can be used with great success all over the house, from the patio to the living area and even in the bedrooms and bathrooms. Far more beautiful than their synthetic counterparts, terra-cotta tiles improve with age. Like their typical surroundings, they are functional and uncontrived while the variations in their natural coloring and texture add a welcome richness and warmth to any room in which they are found.

The shade of a terra-cotta tile can vary dramatically depending on the region from which it originates. Tiles from Provence in France are characterized by their varying shades of warm pink and yellow while those from Tuscany in Italy are ocher. Different clays can be combined and a variety of textural effects obtained by using different types of kilns. Tiles are available in a range of thicknesses and shapes, such as square, hexagonal, rectangular, and octagonal. A common combination is cream and red tiles, which gives a distinctive checkered pattern. However you use terra-cotta tiles, you will appreciate the way they deepen in color and develop a characteristic glowing patina as time goes by.

Ceramic tiles provide a good way of introducing a light and sunny feel to a room, thanks to their bright reflective surface. Cool, hard, and long-lasting, they are water- and usually stain-resistant. In a domestic setting they are most frequently used on a bathroom floor. There is a huge choice of colors, patterns, and shapes available, although it's best to keep the floor design fairly simple unless you are using them to define a specific area, such as the floor

below A simple ceramic bowl is a thing of beauty in itself. Here its harmonizing colors, teamed with a design that counters the design on the tiles, make it a superb accessory.

below Terra-cotta floor tiles vary individually in shade and texture to give an attractively warm yet hard-wearing surface to any room.

above *Tile borders give a satisfactorily clean finish to an area of tiling. Here, a dramatic and cohesive effect is achieved by running horizontal bands of tiles across the lip of the shelf, along the top and bottom of the backsplash, and above the cabinets.*

of a shower. Borders or bands of color can provide a neat finishing touch, tiles can be organized at random, or contrasts can be made by inserting a pattern of bright tiles into a white or other neutral background. Before you do anything too dramatic, consider the size of the room you are tiling. Small tiles, dark colors, and too much going on will make the room seem smaller, whereas larger, brighter, less busy areas of color create a sense of space and light. Ceramic tiles do not age in the graceful way of their terra-cotta counterparts but, provided they are looked after properly, they should retain their fresh, clean look for a long time.

Tiling for walls

The irregularities in shape, texture, and color that come from hand-finishing are typical of Mediterranean walls. Wall tiles are predominantly used in the kitchen and bathroom, as they provide a hygienic surface that is both waterproof and easy to clean, and offer a smoother finish to counteract the rough natural surfaces. Today neither of these rooms has a purely utilitarian function—the kitchen has become the warm heart of the home while the bathroom has become a private sanctuary that is inviting and pleasant to enter.

In kitchens, tiles are commonly used for backsplashes and countertops. Using plain tiles in a delicate aquamarine, a brilliant deep blue, or a cheerful yellow will immediately evoke sunnier climes. More than one color can be used, either in random patterns, in geometric designs, or with a contrasting border. Intersperse rows of plain tiles with occasional patterned ones. Tiles that feature pictures of vegetables, herbs, or fruit, or perhaps culinary terms in French, Italian, or Spanish, can be good fun.

Before you choose your wall tiles, remember that they are a more permanent addition to the room than a coat of paint, so it is particularly important to feel happy with your choice. Look at the rest of the room and decide on your colors carefully. You may need to take into consideration the existing color scheme in the room or the colors of storage jars, china, or any utensils on display. Decide how much of the wall you want to cover. Will the

opposite *Two simple rows of tiles in a contrasting blue that are echoed in the sink transform what could be a chilly niche into an eye-catching corner.*

below *Ceramics and glassware are displayed on characteristic shelves, allowing their differing shapes, colors, and textures to be fully appreciated.*

backsplash just run below the level of the cabinets or reach right up to the ceiling? If the latter, you may want a less overpowering color, depending on the size of the room. If you want to keep the wall space free for pots and pans, inject some life into the room by using tiles across the front of a cooktop hood or along the lip of the countertop. If you are using wall tiles on the counter or around a cooktop or sink, be sure to use bacteria- and water-resistant grout that can be washed clean.

When it comes to the bathroom, tiling is unquestionably the most practical wall covering. It can be used to cover the entire room or just a particular area, such as behind the bath and sink, or over the entire shower area. Use tiles around a mirror, over the counter, or even inside the sink itself.

Splendid effects can be achieved by combining different shapes of tiles in simple geometric designs of two or more colors. Designs that feature seaside subjects such as fish, shells, and waves are particularly appealing and can transform the atmosphere in an instant. Experiment with combinations of different-sized tiles to create original effects. Sheets of aquamarine and blue mosaic tiles are often extremely effective in evoking those clear Mediterranean waters. Strong blues and whites are fresh and cool while warmer effects can be achieved with yellows, blues, terra-cottas, and greens. An area of plain tiles can be topped with a border that creates a focus in the room and makes the ceiling seem lower.

The use of tiles is not limited to the kitchen and bathroom—they can be used in any room as murals or pictures, or even on the exterior walls. Be creative in your approach to tiling and don't restrict yourself to areas of the house traditionally associated with tiles. Use broken tiles to make patterned mosaics on tabletops and stone seats. Frame panels of tiles to hang as pictures or set them into a wall, framed by border tiles. Decorate stairways, both interior and exterior, by tiling the rise of each step. Frame arches and doorways with distinctive tiles. Tile the walls within a window recess to reflect any incoming light and direct attention to the world outside. There are all sorts of ways to brighten your home with tiles. Just let your imagination get to work.

right *Ceramic tiles are the ideal waterproof solution for a bathroom or shower. The light plays on the deep blue floor-to-ceiling tiles, creating a suitably watery but sunny feel.*

Ceramics

Hand-painted ceramic pottery is an essential characteristic of the Mediterranean house. It has been a feature ever since the Islamic craftsmen of the 6th and 7th centuries migrated from their home countries across the sea to Moorish Spain. The pieces are made from clay, which is molded into the required shape and then fired in a kiln. Kilns are usually electric or gas but they can be run on oil or solid fuel. Once the piece has sufficiently hardened, it is ready to be glazed.

The process of making majolica specifically consists of applying a tin enamel that when dry forms an opaque white porous surface. A design is then painted on in glaze and a transparent glaze is applied. Glazes are a mixture of chemical compounds, minerals, and oxides that are otherwise dipped, sprayed, or painted onto the piece. When the piece is fired again, the glazes and colors are fused onto the clay and produce the brightly decorated pieces typical of the Mediterranean region.

Ceramic pottery is used for all sorts of domestic items—plates, serving dishes, lamp bases, urns, candlesticks, cups, bowls, and figurines. Although the objects are of primarily practical use, they are also typically decorative and are frequently on display. If not in use, plates are openly stored in racks by the sink or on shelves. They are used as wall decorations too. Cups can be hung from hooks while bright fruit bowls grace kitchen tables. The distinctive use of vibrant colors and designs, either pictorial or patterned, varies from region to region. Using them in your home is a surefire way of evoking the Mediterranean way of life.

below These two realistic-looking classical urns demonstrate how effectively pictures can be created in tilework to make a strong focal point in a room.

opposite The honeyed tones of the wood are echoed in the tiled motifs that frame the backsplash while the colors of the urns themselves are repeated in the detailing on the cabinets.

In a relaxed, informal setting attuned to nature, furnishings in the Mediterranean home are primarily functional and uncontrived. Made from natural materials and chosen with an eye for its essential beauty, each piece contributes toward an uncluttered, timeless look.

FURNITURE

Furniture for a Mediterranean life

Life in Mediterranean countries slows down to a leisurely pace that is in tune with the seasons. This is reflected in the decoration of the houses of the region. Contents are stripped back to the barest essentials. Each element of furniture used should be a testament to simplicity, the use of natural materials, and a sense of tradition and history.

Simplicity does not mean discomfort—quite the reverse. Furniture should invite relaxation: hours spent chatting around a table, snoozing through a siesta, sitting over a glass of wine or a meal, winding down after a hard day's work. Most importantly, furnishing a Mediterranean-style interior should not be governed by interior design trends or fashion statements. This is no show home. Pieces of furniture do not have to be chosen to fit in a particular decorative scheme but to answer a particular need. Form follows function. Each item has a purpose and a timelessness that gives it an enduring appeal, whether it's a capacious dresser, a sturdy table, or a comfortable sofa. Furniture that has been handed down through generations can connect us to our past and this lends a special atmosphere to the house.

Each room reflects the personalities and habits of the people who live there. The fact that much of life is spent outdoors influences the design of the interior, encouraging the use of natural materials and paying homage to the concept of bringing the outside in. The emphasis on simplicity means that attention is focused on the variety and richness of the textures in a room. The weave of natural fabrics such as cotton, linen, and wool is set against the grain of different woods, the uneven surface of wicker, rattan, or rush, the strong smooth curves of wrought iron, the patterns in the floor covering, rugs, and mats. A home with a Mediterranean-inspired atmosphere depends on the ability to create a comfortable, warm, and inviting setting in which friends and family will feel at ease.

opposite Furniture in the Mediterranean home is not ultra chic or ornate. Unadorned, functional pieces combine over time to produce a natural, unfussy style with an individuality all of its own.

below A heavy carved dresser provides the solution for holding plenty of herbs, spices, and other cooking ingredients or utensils. It is wholly functional, yet the carved detailing gives it a particularly distinctive character.

Living room furniture

As in the rest of the house, the living room is pared down to its basics. The emphasis is on an uncluttered area and the space is left as open and airy as possible. In the summer the focus of the room may turn toward the French doors and the patio or toward a large window that frames a panoramic view. In the winter, it will focus on the fireplace. Originally sited in the kitchen for heating and cooking, the fireplace has become a purely decorative feature, where a roaring log fire provides a feeling of intimacy. Burning pinecones will give off a wonderful aromatic smell. Store them and the logs in large open wicker baskets by the fireplace. There is no place here for endless knick-knacks, elaborate fabrics, and precious or uncomfortable furniture. What you need is a squashy upholstered sofa to lie on or to share with one or two other people, cozy chairs placed near a window as a comfortable spot for reading, and a low coffee table that is perfect as a footrest or as a surface for a game of backgammon or chess.

A solid wooden blanket chest or trunk can make a good substitute for a table. Most Mediterranean houses contain antiques that may have been passed through generations of the family, but a similar effect is possible using pieces bought at flea markets, antiques fairs, or auctions. Garage sale finds can be carefully painted and distressed to fake an impression of age. A sense of nostalgia for times past prevails. Color schemes can vary according to taste and the particular part of the world that is the source of your

above *Terracotta, dusky and pale yellow tones lend themselves very well to the Mediterranean style. A dash of sharp violet adds a complementary but invigorating touch to any room.*

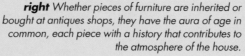

left *A variety of lamps around a room provide a soft background lighting which will successfully disguise any imperfections in their surroundings.*

right *Whether pieces of furniture are inherited or bought at antiques shops, they have the aura of age in common, each piece with a history that contributes to the atmosphere of the house.*

below *Furniture that has been collected over the years may not coordinate exactly but instead it gives a strong impression of comfort and of a family home that has been long loved and looked after.*

inspiration—the subtle, earthy tones of the Tuscan palette or the warm reds, blues, and greens of Provence, for example. If you're a little unsure about experimenting with wall colors to evoke the warmth of the Mediterranean lifestyle, follow the example of the minimalist limewashed white walls of Greece or Spain. It is easy to brighten a white room with colored or patterned chair and sofa covers in vivid yellows, blues, and greens, to conjure up sunny days. Pillow covers can be in a variety of patterns and colors, including the rich and vibrant fabrics used for woven rugs (kilims) from Turkey. By taking the white route, you still have scope to change the feel of the room with the seasons, substituting brighter or more subdued shades to suit the mood. This is far from the world of coordinated decorator fabrics, so chairs can be covered in different materials, shades, textures, and patterns, provided they adhere to a common theme.

Wooden bookshelves, whether built-in or freestanding, display one or two precious objects or items that are reminiscent of the ocean, such as wooden boats or glass fishing balls, as well as books. Bring in the outdoor world and a puff of sea air by using a single piece of driftwood as a sculpture, a plate of shells from the beach, fresh or dried flowers informally arranged in pitchers, or even a potted palm. Although walls frequently go undecorated, one or two carefully hung pictures, a wall hanging, or a couple of ethnic straw hats will help bring the room together to convey the atmosphere of an authentic Mediterranean living room.

Dining room furniture

Meals are a priority in any Mediterranean household and are often eaten in the kitchen (see MEDITERRANEAN KITCHEN) when the family gathers at the beginning and end of the day. Having a separate dining room is less typical and it is likely to be used only in winter when the weather makes eating outside impossible, or for more formal occasions. The only indispensable pieces of furniture are the table and chairs. Large pine farmhouse tables take pride of place. Scrubbed pale and smooth over the years,

opposite *Outdoor furniture can be used just as successfully indoors. There is a long tradition around the Mediterranean of making wrought-iron furniture, which has the benefits of being weatherproof, long-lasting, and attractive.*

below *Mosaic tabletops have a bright, easy-to-clean surface that can become the centerpiece of any room. Their patterns can be organized formally or completely at random, depending on the desired effect.*

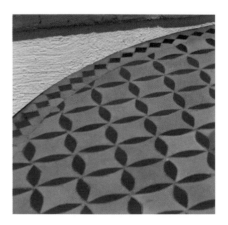

below *It is common to adapt the use of a piece of furniture over the years. An armoire can be ideal for storing china or utensils in the kitchen while an old wooden cradle makes an unusual plant holder.*

they develop a character all of their own, scarred from chopping vegetables or cutting bread. On special occasions, a damask tablecloth or a more informal checked or patterned one can immediately transform the table's appearance.

Some pieces of furniture can be used outside just as well as inside and are frequently interchangeable. Wrought-iron tables and chairs can be adapted for use indoors with the flick of a tablecloth and the addition of some comfy cushions. A tile- or mosaic-topped table is equally adaptable, adding a welcome touch of color to any dining room. Rush-seated chairs are ideal as long as they aren't left out in the rain, otherwise wood or wicker ones make excellent substitutes. Metal chairs, folding or not, are usually painted white or green and are the most adaptable to both inside and outside use. Wood and metal are softened by the use of cushions or slipcovers, which can easily be removed when the weather changes. A glass-fronted cabinet, a dresser, or an old armoire can be used for storing plates, knives, forks, and table linen. Open shelves show off the shapes and designs of your china or pottery. Rush table mats, bread baskets, and cheese trays all add to the Mediterranean feel.

It's common for many dining tables to be lit by a pendant light. If a retractable light is used, it can be as high or low, formal or informal, as the occasion demands. At nighttime, the atmosphere can be softened by a candlelit glow which unfailingly creates a warm and inviting atmosphere appropriate for dining.

below *The unusual construction of the two doors adds an exciting dimension to this room, while echoing the predominantly rustic or Mediterranean feel within.*

right *Distressing furniture to give an impression of age or just painting it plain are both techniques suited to a Mediterranean-inspired interior.*

Bedroom furniture

The bedroom provides a sanctuary far away from the noise and hubbub of the rest of the house. More than anything, it should possess an air of peace, tranquility, and intimacy. It needs to be uncluttered by the trappings of everyday life, so that there is little to distract from the business of relaxation and sleep. White walls immediately lighten the room, adding a greater sense of space and offering few distractions. Muted earth colors give a much warmer, more protective feel. Other than a particular wall hanging or a favorite picture or small decoration, the walls remain largely undecorated. The most important thing in the room is the bed. Traditional wrought-iron or wooden bedsteads make a definitive statement, either through the simplicity of their design or through the more intricate metalwork or wood carving. Occasionally the bed is on a platform within an alcove, and hidden from view by heavy decorative curtains. Covers are cool, natural, and neutral—crisp cotton or linen. Pillows are piled high against the headboard. A throw

opposite Light, airy, and unfussy, this bedroom is a private retreat from the rest of the house. Wicker chairs are complemented by hats on the wall and baskets at the end of the bed. Once again, the watchword is simplicity.

left Natural weave rugs act as a perfect foil to the contrasting textures of wicker and wood in this bedroom. Subtly dyed, they can bring a quiet note of color into the room.

or blanket might provide a splash of color at the foot of the bed. Mosquito nets that billow in the breeze are suspended from a crown above the bed, romantically shrouding it or knotted casually out of the way when not in use. If the bed has a high frame, the mosquito net can be hung from it. To make a stronger, more intimate statement, use the bolder deep reds, blues, and greens of Turkey, set off with a gleam of gold in the thread. Old wooden chests of drawers and wardrobes hide all possessions, while a couple of books, a clock, and a brass lamp sit together on each nightstand with perhaps a simple open shelf for books and candles. An easy chair sits in a corner with the light slanting through the fine cotton curtains, making a quiet spot for reading or sewing. This is a haven of simplicity and rest lit by natural light during the day and by the flicker of candlelight or the glow of an oil lamp in the evening. Bunches of wildflowers freshen the room when in season while bowls of lavender or potpourri add their distinctive perfume.

Bathroom furniture

The bathroom also gives a lot of scope for an imaginative approach to furnishings. Once a room devoted only to hygiene, the bathroom has become a private place for indulging the senses. This is as true in the Mediterranean as anywhere else. Built-in baths and showers are decorated with ceramic tiles, either plain or patterned, depending on the desired effect. A claw-footed rolltop bath can be just as effective, if possible with a view through a window. Again, the watchwords are simple and natural. Fresh cotton towels are piled on open shelves, stacked in a cupboard, or hung on a traditional wooden towel rail. Wooden duckboards or cork bathmats cover cool stone or tiled floors. Wicker baskets contain soaps and rolls of toilet paper. Fresh flowers or plants that enjoy a steamy atmosphere lend a striking color contrast while scented candles perfume the air. For something more exotic, tile the walls in cobalt, turquoise, and gold mosaic. Marble every surface. Let the light from a lantern play on the dark ceiling and add palms or ferns as a finishing touch.

Whatever your taste in furnishings, there is a region of the Mediterranean that will inspire you to re-create its essence within your home.

right *This sea-green bathroom, with its churchlike window, features some interesting furnishings. The chair, in untreated wood, helps give the room an organic feel and the unusual green and gold mirror frame adds interest.*

PICTURE CREDITS

The author and publisher would like to thank Elizabeth Whiting Associates and the following photographers and organizations for their kind permission to reproduce photographs on the following pages: 2, 17, 51, 61, 69 Andreas von Einsiedel; 7, 11, 34-5, 42, 65, 95 Di Lewis; 8, 27, 29, 41 Lu Jeffrey; 9, 16 Nadia MacKenzie; 10 Tim Street-Porter; 13, 28, 47, 70-1, 76 EWA; 14-15, 19, 22-3, 72, 79, 88(bottom) 89 Steve Sparrow; 20-1, 66 David Markson; 24-5, 74-5 Michael Dunne; 30-1 Dennis Stone; 32-3 Peter Aprahamian; 36, 52-3 Nick Carter; 37, 55-9, 62-3, 73, 77, 86-7, 90-1, 93 Peter Woloszynska; 38, 46 Mark Thomas; 43, 74(bottom) Fired Earth; 44-5, 83 Simon Upton; 48-9, 80-1, 95 Brian Harrison; 50 Huntley Hedworth; 67 Adrian Taylor; 84-5 Tom Leighton; 88(top) The Tile Gallery; 92 Mark Luscombe-Whyte.